Egg Cookbook

Easy and Fun Ways to Cook Your Eggs

BY

Julia Chiles

Copyright 2021 - Julia Chiles

License Notes

No part of this Book can be reproduced in any form or by any means including print, electronic, scanning or photocopying unless prior permission is granted by the author.

All ideas, suggestions and guidelines mentioned here are written for informative purposes. While the author has taken every possible step to ensure accuracy, all readers are advised to follow information at their own risk. The author cannot be held responsible for personal and/or commercial damages in case of misinterpreting and misunderstanding any part of this Book

Table of Contents

Introduction 6

    Sausage and Egg Tacos 9

    Cauliflower Egg Salad 11

    Creamy Broccoli and Cauliflower Egg Salad 13

    Egg Salad with Shrimp 15

    Cilantro Egg Salad 17

    Cheesy Potato Frittata 19

    Herbed Tomato Frittata with Feta 21

    Pepper Tomato and Cheese Frittata 23

    Parmesan Zucchini Eggs 25

    Eggs in Bread 27

    Fried Sausage and Eggs 29

    Tomato Feta Eggs 31

    Eggs from France 33

    Deviled Egg Salad 35

    Scrambled Eggs with Tuna and Alfalfa 37

    Romano and Pepperoni Eggs 39

    Scrambled Eggs with Pepper Tomato and Garlic 41

    Spinach Tomato and Cheese Frittata 43

    Macaroni and Eggs Florentine Style 45

Herbed Tuna and Spinach Frittata 47

Tuna Egg Salad 49

Leftover Salmon and Cherry Tomato Quiche 51

Scrambled Eggs Done Right 54

Curry Mango Chutney Egg Salad 56

Vegetarian Eggs 58

Chicken and Vegetable Quiche with Mozzarella 60

Scrambled Eggs with Sun-Dried Tomatoes on Toast 63

Spinach Ricotta and Herb Quiche 65

Eggs Florentine 68

Fried Eggs and Shrimp 70

Omelet 72

Cheesy Broccoli and Onion Quiche 74

Chipotle Bacon and Eggs 77

Avocado Egg Salad 79

Breakfast Eggs from India 81

Paprika Egg Salad 83

Chicken Egg Salad 85

Gherkins Egg Salad 87

Easy Spicy Eggs 89

Buttery Eggs 91

Chicken Ham Pepper and Cheese Omelette 93

Simply the Best Egg Salad 95

Quick Pickled Eggs with Beets 97

Scrambled Eggs with Tomato and Paprika 99

Curried Deviled Eggs 101

Cloud Eggs 103

French Toast 105

Spinach Quiche 107

Vegetable Frittata 109

Huevos Rancheros 112

Beef Egg Salad 115

Breakfast Biscuits 117

Smoked Salmon Egg Salad 119

Chakchouka 121

Mustard Pickled Eggs 124

Irresistible Scotch Eggs 126

Egg Salad Sandwiches 128

Cheesy Egg Whites in a Mug 130

Conclusion 132

Author's Afterthoughts 133

Introduction

Come on in! We want to introduce you to the best way to raise eggs. Eggs are a great source of protein, but few people realize that they are also an excellent source of valuable nutrients. Here's how you can use eggs to help make your family healthier and happier.

Eggs are one of the most versatile foods available. They're perfect for breakfast, lunch, and dinner. And they're a great way to increase your protein intake without adding extra weight. But what do eggs have to do with carpentry? And why would you want to cook with them?

You've probably heard that eggs provide a great source of protein. In fact, an egg contains more than 6 grams of protein in a single serving. That's more than any other source of protein, such as meat or cheese. Protein is essential for building and repairing muscles, making healthy hair and nails, nourishing the stomach, and much more.

Start your day with a smile. And one of the big, juicy, beautiful eggs at the ready! This cookbook is the perfect breakfast companion. Besides being a healthy way to start your day, it's an easy preparation that can be used for a variety of other dishes that would not be possible without eggs. But don't stop there; their versatility means they can be used to create delicious recipes that'll keep you on the go all day long!

We've all heard it a million times. "Eggs are good for you!" To be quite honest, it's true. We offer a wealth of healthy recipes in our cookbook, from breakfasts to desserts.

The trick to making the perfect omelet is all about the ingredients you choose. We've made it easy for you to choose the right ingredients to make a healthy and hearty breakfast.

Eggs are an incredibly versatile ingredient that can be used to make a variety of dishes. The high level of protein and vitamins in eggs are great for breakfast, snacks, and even desserts.

If you're looking for some delicious breakfast ideas, turn to the cookbook for all your egg recipe needs. From pancakes to frittatas, we've got you covered. No matter what time of day it is, the recipes will be sure to put a smile on your face.

But just because eggs are healthy, it doesn't mean they're easy to make. It's not unusual for someone new to cooking to get frustrated when things don't come out as they thought they would. That is where our cookbook comes in. We offer a wide variety of techniques that will make cooking eggs much easier and more enjoyable than they ever were before.

Eggs are one of the four food groups, but that doesn't mean you should eat them every day. In moderation, eggs can create a healthy snack or meal. Our cookbook covers everything from omelets and breakfasts to egg-based desserts and snacks. Each recipe is simple yet flavorful.

You can use the cookbook to treat yourself or share with family and friends. Whether you're an expert chef or a beginner, you'll be amazed at how easy it is to cook with eggs. And who knows? You might even decide that they're good for you after all!

Get ready to pick up a pan and fry up some eggs! The egg cookbook includes a wide variety of delicious egg dishes that are good for breakfast, lunch and dinner. You can make any of the recipes in your own kitchen in no time flat. They are the best egg recipes around.

Egg Recipes

There are a lot of reasons why people enjoy eating breakfast eggs: they're inexpensive, they're flexible, and they're filled with protein that's good for you, which means they're great for a strong start to your day. Eggs are also versatile when it comes to cooking. Here are some of the tasty dishes you can make with our versatile egg product:

Sausage and Egg Tacos

There's no reason you can't have both eggs and sausages for breakfast occasionally.

Servings: 3

Preparation Time: 15 minutes

Ingredients:

- 2 tbsp. butter
- ¼ c. chopped red peppers
- 1 chopped and seeded jalapeno pepper
- 1 small diced onion
- 1/3 c. shredded Swiss cheese
- 6 beaten eggs
- Salt and pepper to taste
- ½ c. cooked and crumbled sausages
- Salt and pepper to taste
- 6 corn tortillas

Directions:

1. Heat the butter in a skillet.

2. Sauté the red pepper and jalapeno pepper and onion for 5 minutes.

3. Pour the beaten eggs and sausages over the vegetables and keep stirring until the eggs are scrambled about 5 minutes.

4. Season with salt and pepper.

5. Add the shredded cheese and remove from heat. Keep warm.

6. Bake the tortillas in the oven for 5 minutes at 350 degrees.

7. Spoon the filling into the tortillas and fold in half.

Cauliflower Egg Salad

For all egg salad lovers who also love cauliflower. If you're looking for a great way to use up your leftover cauliflower, you can try this recipe. You can eat it during lunch or dinner, and it's delicious!

Servings: 6

Preparation Time: 1 hour and 30 minutes

Ingredients:

- 1 large head cauliflower, chopped and steamed
- 4 hard-boiled eggs, chopped
- 1 c. mayonnaise
- 2 stalks celery, diced
- 4 chopped green onions
- ¼ c. sour cream
- 2 tbsp. apple cider vinegar
- 1 tsp. white sugar
- Salt and black pepper to taste

Directions:

1. Place all ingredients in a large bowl and mix until thoroughly combined.

2. Chill at least 1 hour before serving.

3. Serve and enjoy.

Creamy Broccoli and Cauliflower Egg Salad

For all egg salad lovers that also love cauliflower, this is the time with a twist of broccoli as well. Great to make ahead for a healthy on the go-to breakfast. You can even make this recipe with leftover vegetables.

Servings: 6

Preparation Time: 1 hour and 30 minutes

Ingredients:

- 1 large head cauliflowers, chopped and steamed
- 1 large head broccoli, chopped and steamed
- 4 hard-boiled eggs
- 1 c. mayonnaise, miracle whip can be used if preferred
- 2 stalks celery, diced
- 4 chopped green onions
- ¼ c. sour cream
- 2 tbsp. apple cider vinegar
- 1 tsp. white sugar
- Salt and black pepper to taste

Directions:

1. Place all ingredients in a large bowl and mix until completely combined.

2. Chill at least 1 hour before serving.

3. Serve and enjoy.

Egg Salad with Shrimp

Shrimp goes well with an egg salad. This is a delicious and quick shrimp salad recipe with a touch of egg. Take your time to make the shrimp.

Servings: 4

Preparation Time: 15 minutes

Ingredients:

- 4 hard-boiled eggs, chopped
- 4 tbsp. mayonnaise
- 1 lb. cooked Shrimp, peeled, deveined, and chopped
- 1 sprig dill, chopped
- 1 tsp. Dijon Mustard
- 4 leaves green lettuce

Directions:

1. Place all ingredients, except lettuce, in a large bowl and mix until completely combined. Serve on a lettuce leaf and enjoy.

Cilantro Egg Salad

Cilantro is an excellent ingredient to have in an egg salad. A great salad for any time of the day. You can use fresh cracked eggs and mayonnaise instead of egg salad dressing.

Servings: 6

Preparation Time: 20 minutes

Ingredients:

- 5 hard-boiled eggs, finely chopped
- ¾ c. mayonnaise
- ¾ chopped cilantro
- 1 tbsp. Dijon mustard
- 1 tsp. lemon juice
- 1 tsp. lime juice
- 1 stalk celery, finely diced
- 4 mushrooms, finely diced
- Salt and black pepper

Directions:

1. Place all ingredients in a large bowl and mix until completely combined.

Cheesy Potato Frittata

In this simple and delicious frittata, there are so many delicious things going on. The recipe blends potatoes and onions with custard eggs borrowed from the classic tortilla Española (aka Spanish tortilla) form. The frittata is great to make ahead and reheat for a quick breakfast.

Servings: 6

Preparation Time: 30 minutes

Ingredients:

- 2 tbsp. olive oil
- 1 medium white onion, sliced
- 2 new potatoes, thinly sliced (about 200g each)
- 4 whole eggs
- 4 egg whites
- 1/3 c. milk
- 1/2 c. cheddar cheese, shredded
- Salt and freshly ground black pepper

Directions:

1. Preheat your broiler.

2. In a large oven-proof pan, heat olive oil over medium flame. Stir-fry the onion for 2-3 minutes or until aromatic.

3. Add the potatoes, cover, and cook for 15-20 minutes or until tender but firm.

4. Meanwhile, beat together the eggs and milk in a medium bowl. Season to taste. Then pour it into the pan over the potatoes and sprinkle with cheddar cheese. Turn the heat to low, cover with a lid, and cook for about 3 minutes.

5. Place the pan in the broiler and cook for 5 minutes or until set and the top is golden brown.

6. Serve and enjoy.

Herbed Tomato Frittata with Feta

This is a great brunch recipe for a crowd. You can use any vegetables in your fridge. An oven-proof nonstick pan is the key to the recipe, which helps the eggs to properly cook, prevents them from sticking, and reduces cleanup.

Servings: 5

Preparation Time: 30 minutes

Ingredients:

- 2 tbsp. olive oil
- 2 cloves garlic, minced
- 1 shallot, chopped
- 2 tomatoes, chopped
- 6 whole eggs
- 1/4 c. milk
- 2 tbsp. heavy cream
- 1/2 c. feta cheese, crumbled
- 1 tbsp. dill weed, chopped
- Salt and freshly ground black pepper

Directions:

1. Preheat and set your oven to 400 F (200 C).

2. In a large oven-proof pan, heat olive oil over medium flame. Stir-fry shallot, garlic, and tomatoes for 2-3 minutes or until aromatic and soft.

3. Meanwhile, beat together the eggs, milk, and cream in a medium bowl. Season to taste. Pour into the pan over the vegetables. Top with crumbled feta and sprinkle with dill. Turn the heat to low, cover with a lid, and cook for about 3 minutes.

4. Transfer pan into the oven and bake for 8-10 minutes or until set and golden brown.

5. Serve and enjoy.

Pepper Tomato and Cheese Frittata

For those looking for a low carb breakfast, this frittata is for you. It is an easy dish to make, and it can be anything you want.

Servings: 6

Preparation Time: 35 minutes

Ingredients:

- 2 tbsp. olive oil
- 2 shallots, chopped
- 1 tsp. garlic, minced
- 1/2 medium yellow bell pepper, deseeded and diced
- 1/2 medium red bell pepper, deseeded and diced
- 1/2 c. grape tomatoes, diced
- 5 whole eggs
- 4 egg whites
- 3 tbsp. half and half cream
- 1/3 c. cheddar cheese, grated
- Salt and freshly ground black pepper

Directions:

1. Preheat your broiler.

2. In an oven-proof pan, start heating the olive oil over medium flame. Add the shallots and garlic, stir-fry for 2-3 minutes or until aromatic.

3. Add the peppers and tomatoes; cook for 3-5 minutes, stirring occasionally.

4. Meanwhile, whisk together the eggs and cream in a medium bowl. Season to taste. Pour egg mixture over the peppers and tomatoes, then sprinkle with cheese. Turn the heat to low, cover with a lid, and cook for 2-3 minutes.

5. Transfer the pan into the broiler and cook further 5 minutes or until set and golden brown.

6. Serve and enjoy.

Parmesan Zucchini Eggs

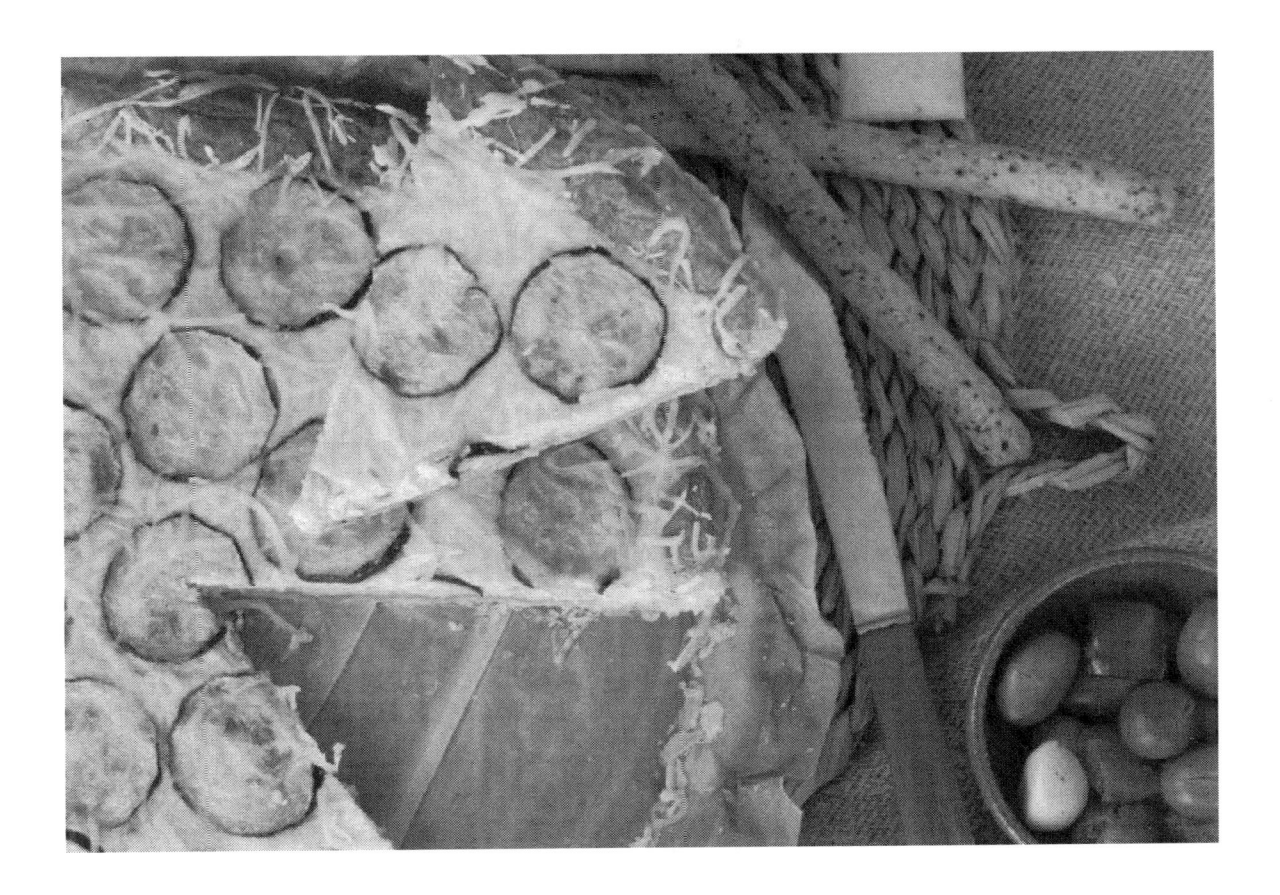

While summer is a peak season, zucchini is available throughout the year; just make sure to pick out the best-looking. Have a side of vegetables with this egg breakfast dish. The dish is gluten free, and you can adjust the amount of cheese to your preference.

Servings: 4

Preparation Time: 35 minutes

Ingredients:

- 4 eggs, lightly beaten
- Garlic powder to taste
- 2 tbsp. grated Parmesan cheese
- Salt and ground black pepper to taste
- 2 tbsp. olive oil
- 1 zucchini, sliced 1/8- to 1/4-inch thick

Directions:

1. Get a bowl, evenly mix: parmesan and whisked eggs.

2. Get a 2nd small bowl, combine in pepper, garlic powder, and salt.

3. Fry your zucchini in olive oil for 8 minutes. Pour in the seasonings from the 2nd bowl.

4. Lower the heat and pour in the first bowl.

5. Cook eggs for 4 mins. Turn off the heat and place a lid on the pan for 2 minutes until the eggs are completely done.

Eggs in Bread

A perfect way to enjoy an egg in a slightly different way is a delicious runny yolk egg fried in the middle of a slice of toast eaten with a fork. When eating it, kids feel fancy.

Servings: 1

Preparation Time: 30 minutes

Ingredients:

- 1/2 tbsp. butter
- 1 slice white bread
- 1 egg

Directions:

1. Coat your bread with butter on each of its sides. Then, cut-out a circle in the middle of it.

2. Whisk your egg in a small bowl. Set it aside.

3. Get a skillet hot and for 1 min fry each side of the bread. Pour the egg into the hole and cook for 3 more mins.

4. Enjoy.

Fried Sausage and Eggs

There are so many ways to enjoy this breakfast dish! You can serve it with a biscuit or toast, or even with pita bread. This is a great scramble of scrambled eggs, cheese, and sausage bits. Good for a family breakfast on a reuniting morning! For the recipe, you can use as much of whatever kind of cheese you prefer.

Servings: 4

Preparation Time: 50 minutes

Ingredients:

- 1 lb. beef sausage meat
- 1/8 tsp. ground black pepper
- 2 tsp. Worcestershire sauce
- 1 egg, whisked
- 4 hard-cooked eggs, peeled
- 2/3 c. dry bread crumbs
- 1 tbsp. all-purpose flour
- 1 quart oil for deep frying
- 1/8 tsp. salt

Directions:

1. Get a bowl, evenly mix Worcestershire, pepper, sausage, salt and flour. Split the mix into four parts.

2. Wrap each of the four eggs with an equal part of the sausage mix.

3. Get 2 bowls. Put whisked eggs into one bowl and crumbled bread into another bowl. Coat each wrapped egg first with whisked eggs, then dip into the bread.

4. Get some oil hot to 365 degrees in a large skillet, saucepan, or fryer and cook the eggs in the oil for 6 minutes.

Tomato Feta Eggs

This is a great side dish for any breakfast or lunch. The recipe is easy to make, and it's really delicious.

Servings: 4

Preparation Time: 25 minutes

Ingredients:

- 1 tbsp. butter
- 2 tbsp. crumbled feta cheese
- 1/4 c. chopped onion
- Salt and pepper to taste
- 4 eggs, beaten
- 1/4 c. chopped tomatoes

Directions:

1. Fry onions until see-through, in butter, in a frying pan. Then, mix in your eggs. While the eggs are frying, make sure to stir them so that they become scrambled.

2. Before the eggs are completely cooked, add in your pepper and salt, then your feta, and finally your tomatoes.

3. Continue to let the eggs fry until the feta melts.

Eggs from France

Improve your simple breakfast with this recipe for creamy eggs. Easter is just around the corner, so go ahead and have it! It is easy to make, and it tastes great.

Servings: 8

Preparation Time: 40 minutes

Ingredients:

- 1/2 c. butter
- 8 hard-cooked eggs
- 1/2 c. flour
- 1 pinch paprika
- Salt and pepper to taste
- 1 quart milk
- 8 slices white bread, toasted

Directions:

1. First, get a saucepan hot before doing anything else.

2. Enter your butter into the saucepan and let it melt completely.

3. Then, add in your flour, stir it a bit, and let it cook for 10 minutes until it becomes lighter in color.

4. Mix in your milk and wait until everything is lightly boiling, then set the heat to low.

5. Let it cook for 10 more minutes.

6. Add in some pepper and salt.

7. Remove the yolks from each egg. Then, you want to dice the egg whites and mix them into the simmering sauce.

8. Get a strainer and press the eggs through it. Put this in a bowl.

9. Put half a cup of simmering sauce on a piece of toasted bread and garnish the bread with the yolks and some paprika.

10. Enjoy.

Deviled Egg Salad

Deviled eggs are a great addition to any meal. You can use hard boiled eggs or soft boiled eggs. This recipe is simple and quick to make, but it tastes great!

Servings: 4

Preparation Time: 25 minutes

Ingredients:

- 12 hard-boiled eggs, chopped
- ¼ c. green onion, chopped
- ½ c. celery
- ½ c. red bell pepper, chopped
- 1/3 c. mayonnaise
- 3 tbsp. Dijon mustard
- 1 tbsp. Sherry or white wine vinegar
- Few drops Tabasco or any hot sauce
- ¼ tsp. paprika
- Salt and black pepper to taste

Directions:

1. Place all ingredients in a large bowl and mix until completely combined.

2. Chill at least 1 hour before serving. Serve and enjoy.

Scrambled Eggs with Tuna and Alfalfa

This is a great side dish. You can serve it with a side of toast or tortillas. The scrambled egg is a recipe for breakfast eggs using chopped onion, canned tuna and olive oil to mix. It is a recipe that is plain, nutritious, and pleasant to Keto, which is low in carbs.

Servings: 4

Preparation Time: 20 minutes

Ingredients:

- 4 whole eggs
- 3 egg whites
- 3 tbsp. half and half cream
- 2 tbsp. olive oil
- 1 medium onion, chopped
- 1 tsp. garlic, minced
- 6 oz. canned tuna flakes in water, drained
- 1/4 tsp. dried dill
- 1/4 tsp. dried thyme
- 1 c. alfalfa sprouts
- Salt and freshly ground black pepper

Directions:

1. First, whisk together the eggs and cream in a medium bowl.

2. Heat oil in a non-stick pan or skillet over medium flame. Stir-fry onion and garlic until aromatic, about 2-3 minutes.

3. Put the tuna flakes, dill, and thyme; cook for 2-3 minutes, stirring occasionally.

4. Next, pour the beaten egg mixture into the pan; cook, often stirring for 2-3 minutes or to desired doneness. Then, season to taste.

5. Then, transfer to a serving dish and top with alfalfa sprouts.

6. Serve and enjoy.

Romano and Pepperoni Eggs

A different way to enjoy hard boiled eggs. You can use the eggs as an appetizer or snack. It's quick and easy to prepare this recipe. We enjoy playing with various breakfast ingredients. One of our favorites is the recipe.

Servings: 2

Preparation Time: 30 minutes

Ingredients:

- 1 c. egg substitute
- 1 tsp. melted butter
- 1 egg
- 1/4 c. grated Romano cheese
- 3 green onions, thinly sliced
- 1 pinch salt and ground black pepper to taste
- 8 slices pepperoni, diced
- 1/2 tsp. garlic powder

Directions:

1. Get a bowl, evenly mix the following in order: garlic powder, egg substitute, pepperoni, green onions, and egg.

2. Fry your eggs in melted butter in a covered frying pan with low heat for 14 mins.

3. Before serving, garnish with Romano cheese and pepper and salt.

4. Enjoy.

Scrambled Eggs with Pepper Tomato and Garlic

For a fast and satisfying egg dish that only takes a few minutes to produce, refrigerated or frozen egg products and fat-free milk join forces with colorful vegetables. You only need a few ingredients to make this delicious dish, and it tastes great for breakfast, lunch, or dinner.

Servings: 4

Preparation Time: 20 minutes

Ingredients:

- 4 whole eggs
- 2 egg whites
- 3 tbsp. milk
- 2 tbsp. olive oil
- 1 tsp. garlic, minced
- 2 medium tomatoes, chopped
- 1/2 medium green bell pepper, deseeded and chopped
- 1/2 medium red bell pepper, deseeded and chopped
- 1 tsp. cayenne pepper powder
- 1/4 tsp. dried basil
- Salt and freshly ground black pepper

Directions:

1. First, whisk together the eggs and milk in a medium bowl.

2. Heat oil in a large non-stick pan or skillet over medium-high flame. Stir-fry garlic for 2-3 minutes.

3. Add the tomatoes, peppers, and dried basil; cook for 2-3 minutes, stirring occasionally.

4. Next, pour the egg mixture into the pan; cook, often stirring for 2-3 minutes or to desired doneness. Then, season to taste.

5. Then, transfer to a serving dish.

6. Serve and enjoy.

Spinach Tomato and Cheese Frittata

The joy of frittata creation is simple, nutritious, and serves an alternative purpose. Frittatas are a versatile dish. You can use any vegetables in your fridge, and you can always add cheese to make them even better. Use hash browns or whatever else you have on hand for the base of this dish.

Servings: 4

Preparation Time: 25 minutes

Ingredients:

- 2 tbsp. olive oil
- 1 shallot, chopped
- 1 tsp. garlic, minced
- 1/4 tsp. dried thyme
- 2 c. baby spinach
- 1 c. cherry tomatoes
- 6 whole eggs
- 1/3 c. low-fat milk
- 1/4 c. mozzarella cheese, grated
- Salt and freshly ground black pepper

Directions:

1. Preheat and set your oven to 400 F (200 C).

2. Heat the oil in an oven-proof pan or skillet over a flame. Sauté the shallot and garlic for 2-3 minutes or until fragrant.

3. Add the spinach and cook for 2 minutes or until wilted.

4. Whisk together the eggs and milk in a mixing bowl. Season to taste.

5. Pour the egg mixture over sautéed spinach, and cook for about 3 minutes or until the edges start to brown. Sprinkle with mozzarella and top with cherry tomatoes.

6. Place the pan inside the oven and cook for 10 minutes more or until the center is set.

7. Serve and enjoy.

Macaroni and Eggs Florentine Style

This is a simple and delicious Florentine egg recipe. Ensure it is not overcooked! This is another great dish that you can make with leftover vegetables. It's an easy and quick dish. Add your favorite pasta and enjoy!

Servings: 3

Preparation Time: 30 minutes

Ingredients:

- 2 tbsp. butter
- Salt and ground black pepper to taste
- 1/2 c. mushrooms, sliced
- 3 tbsp. cream cheese, cut into small pieces
- 2 cloves garlic, minced
- 1/2 (10 oz.) package fresh spinach
- 6 large eggs, slightly beaten

Directions:

1. Fry your garlic and mushrooms in melted butter in a frying pan for 2 minutes. Then, mix in your spinach and cook this for another 4 minutes.

2. Finally, add some pepper and salt and your eggs to the mix and let the eggs set completely. Once the eggs have set you want to flip them.

3. Add a bit of cream cheese to the eggs and let it cook for about 4 minutes.

Herbed Tuna and Spinach Frittata

This tuna frittata is an egg dish that is fried. It consists of canned tuna, butter and beaten eggs. I love getting it with toast or muffins for breakfast. This is a delicious and healthy dish that you can serve with a side of veggies for extra points!

Servings: 5

Preparation Time: 35 minutes

Ingredients:

- 1 medium red onion, chopped
- 2 cloves garlic, minced
- 6 oz. canned tuna in water, flaked
- 2 c. baby spinach
- 4 whole eggs
- 4 egg whites
- 1/3 c. milk
- 2 tbsp. fresh basil, chopped
- 2 tbsp. fresh parsley, chopped
- 2 tbsp. olive oil
- Salt and freshly ground black pepper

Directions:

1. Preheat your broiler.

2. Next, in a large oven-proof pan, heat olive oil over medium flame. Add the onion and garlic, stir-fry for 2-3 minutes or until fragrant.

3. Add tuna, spinach, basil, and parsley. Cook for 3-5 minutes, stirring occasionally.

4. Meanwhile, whisk together the eggs and milk in a medium bowl. Season to taste then pour over the tuna and spinach in the pan. Turn the heat to low, cover with lid, and cook for 2-3 minutes.

5. Then, place the pan in the broiler and cook for another 5 minutes or until set and golden brown.

6. Serve and enjoy.

Tuna Egg Salad

One who appreciates an egg salad will love tuna as well. If you're looking for a great lunch or dinner option, you can try this delicious recipe. It's quick and easy to make.

Servings: 8

Preparation Time: 30 minutes

Ingredients:

- 1 can (15 oz.) tuna (tuna in water)
- 8 hard-boiled eggs, chopped)
- 1 medium onion, diced
- 1 tsp. ground mustard
- 1 dash Dijon mustard
- 2 tsp. Paprika
- 2 tbsp. mayonnaise, or to taste
- Salt and black pepper to taste

Directions:

1. Place all ingredients in a large bowl and mix until completely combined. Serve and enjoy.

Leftover Salmon and Cherry Tomato Quiche

A tasty, healthy and vibrant quiche, full of goodness and sugar-friendly in your blood. This is a great way to use up leftover salmon or leftover cherry tomatoes. You can add some cheese and spinach if you want a heartier dish.

Servings: 2

Preparation Time: 5 minutes

Ingredients:

- 2 tbsp. olive oil
- 1 medium red onion, chopped
- 1 tsp. garlic, minced
- 1 c. cherry tomatoes, halved
- 10 oz. leftover baked salmon, cut into thin strips
- 1 tsp. dill weed, chopped
- 1 (9 inches) pie crust, unbaked
- 1/3 c. cheddar cheese, grated
- 2 tbsp. parmesan, grated
- 6 whole eggs
- 4 egg whites
- 2/3 c. milk
- 1/2 tsp. kosher salt
- 1/2 tsp. lemon pepper

Directions:

1. Preheat and set your oven to 350 F (175 C).

2. Heat oil in a large non-stick pan or skillet over medium flame. Then, add the onion and garlic, stir-fry for about 2-3 minutes.

3. Next, add the cherry tomatoes; cook, occasionally stirring until soft.

4. Add the salmon and dill; mix well. Remove from heat.

5. Transfer the vegetable-salmon mixture onto the pie crust. Sprinkle with cheddar and parmesan.

6. Whisk the eggs in a medium bowl and stir in milk. Season with salt and lemon pepper.

7. Then, pour the egg mixture into the pie crust. Bake in the preheated oven for about 30 to 40 minutes or until the center has set fully.

8. Cool the quiche slightly before serving.

9. Enjoy.

Scrambled Eggs Done Right

The best way for eggs to scramble. A basic recipe to make scrambled eggs the right way. This simple egg dish is great for breakfast or any time of the day. Only mixing and cooking eggs is more than that! This is going to produce a believer out of you.

Servings: 1

Preparation Time: 15 minutes

Ingredients:

- 3 large eggs
- Olive oil
- 1 pinch red pepper flakes
- 1 pinch sea salt
- 9 cherry tomatoes, halved
- 2 tbsp. crumbled feta cheese
- 1 tbsp. very thinly sliced fresh basil leaves

Directions:

1. Get a bowl and evenly mix the following: basil, eggs, feta, red pepper flakes, and tomatoes.

2. Fry in hot olive oil for a few seconds without any stirring, so the eggs are set. Then, begin to scramble them for 1 min.

3. Ideally, you want your eggs to be only lightly set. Remove them from the heat. Season with salt.

4. Enjoy.

Curry Mango Chutney Egg Salad

When you're looking for a great quick and healthy meal option, this egg salad recipe might be right up your alley. It's easy to make, and it tastes great!

Servings: 4

Preparation Time: 25 minutes

Ingredients:

- 6 hard-boiled eggs, chopped
- ½ c. mango chutney
- 1 ½ tsp. yellow curry powder
- ¼ c. celery
- 1 tbsp. mayonnaise
- 1 tbsp. chives
- 1 tbsp. green onion
- 1 tbsp. shallots
- Cayenne, salt, and black pepper to taste

Directions:

1. Place all ingredients in a large bowl and mix until completely combined.

2. Chill at least 1 hour before serving. Serve and enjoy.

Vegetarian Eggs

These vegetarian eggs are quick and easy to make. You can serve the dish during lunch, dinner, and even brunch.

Servings: 6

Preparation Time: 35 minutes

Ingredients:

- 1/4 c. olive oil
- 1/4 c. milk
- 1/4 c. sliced fresh mushrooms
- 1/4 c. chop fresh tomato
- 1/4 c. chop onions
- 1/4 c. shredded Cheddar cheese
- 1/4 c. chop green bell peppers
- 6 eggs

Directions:

1. Get a bowl mix: milk, eggs, and veggies with tomatoes.

2. Fry onions, mushrooms, and peppers until the onions are see-through in hot olive oil in a frying pan.

3. Then, pour in eggs and veggies continue cooking until the eggs are firm.

4. Right before everything is finished, top the eggs with your cheese and cook for another minute.

5. Enjoy.

Chicken and Vegetable Quiche with Mozzarella

For a perfectly sliced breakfast or lunch dish, this plain and springy quiche blends shredded roast chicken leftovers with cheese. The combination of chicken, vegetables, and mozzarella cheese is a delicious addition to the quiche recipe.

Servings: 8

Preparation Time: 1 hour and 10 minutes

Ingredients:

- 2 tbsp. olive oil
- 1 medium red onion, chopped
- 1 tsp. garlic, minced
- 8 oz. leftover roasted chicken, shredded
- 1 c. frozen mixed vegetables, thawed
- 1 tbsp. fresh rosemary, chopped
- 1 tbsp. fresh parsley, chopped
- 1 (10 inches) pie crust, unbaked
- 6 whole eggs
- 4 egg whites
- 3/4 c. milk
- 1/2 c. mozzarella cheese, grated
- 1/2 tsp. kosher salt
- 1/2 tsp. lemon pepper

Directions:

1. Preheat and set your oven to 350 F (175 C).

2. Heat oil in a large non-stick pan or skillet over medium flame. Then, add the onion and garlic, stir-fry for about 2-3 minutes.

3. Next, add the chicken, mixed vegetables, rosemary, and parsley; cook for about 3 minutes, stirring occasionally. Remove from the heat and spoon mixture over the pie crust. Set aside.

4. Whisk together the eggs and milk in a medium bowl. Season with salt and lemon pepper.

5. Then, pour the egg mixture over the chicken and mixed vegetables. Bake in the oven for 20-25 minutes.

6. Sprinkle with mozzarella and cook for another 15-20 minutes.

7. Cool the quiche slightly before serving.

8. Enjoy.

Scrambled Eggs with Sun-Dried Tomatoes on Toast

With sun-dried tomatoes, onion, and Italian herbs, delicious, fluffy scrambled eggs, this is another great dish when you're looking for something different to make for breakfast. It's quick and easy to prepare, and it tastes great! Serve warm with artisan multigrain toast.

Servings: 4

Preparation Time: 20 minutes

Ingredients:

- 3 whole eggs
- 3 egg whites
- 1/4 c. milk
- 2 tbsp. olive oil
- 1 medium white onion, chopped
- 2 tbsp. sun dried tomatoes in oil, drained and chopped
- 2 tbsp. parmesan cheese, grated
- 2 tbsp. fresh basil, chopped
- 4 wholegrain or multigrain bread slices (about 30 g each), toasted
- Salt and freshly ground black pepper
- Fresh basil, for garnish

Directions:

1. Whisk the eggs and stir in milk in a medium bowl.

2. Heat oil in a large non-stick pan or skillet over medium flame. Stir-fry onion and sun-dried tomatoes for 2-3 minutes.

3. Pour the egg mixture, basil, and parmesan; cook, stirring for 2-3 minutes.

4. Spoon about 3 tbsp. of egg mixture on top of each toast and garnish with fresh basil.

5. Serve and enjoy!

Spinach Ricotta and Herb Quiche

Spinach, ricotta cheese, eggs, tomatoes and basil make up this simple vegetarian quiche recipe. A savory breakfast quiche that's great for brunch. You can make the recipe in advance and place it in the fridge to enjoy later.

Servings: 8

Preparation Time: 1 hour and 10 minutes

Ingredients:

- 2 tbsp. butter
- 1/3 c. shallots, chopped
- 1 tsp. garlic, minced
- 3 c. baby spinach
- 1/4 tsp. dried basil
- 1/4 tsp. dried oregano
- 1 (9x9 inches) pie crust, unbaked
- 5 whole eggs
- 4 egg whites
- 1 c. ricotta cheese
- 1/4 c. milk
- Freshly ground black pepper

Directions:

1. Preheat and set your oven to 350 F (175 C). Put the crust in a baking dish.

2. Heat oil in a large non-stick pan or skillet over medium flame. Add the shallots and garlic, stir-fry for 2-3 minutes.

3. Add the spinach, basil, and oregano. Cook for about 2-3 minutes, stirring occasionally. Remove from heat. Spoon vegetables onto the pie crust.

4. Whisk together the eggs, ricotta, and milk in a medium bowl. Season with pepper to taste.

5. Pour the egg mixture over vegetables, spreading evenly. Bake in the preheated oven for about 35-40 minutes or until the center is set fully.

6. Cool the quiche slightly before cutting into portions.

7. Serve and enjoy.

Eggs Florentine

A traditional English dish, this recipe is a great way to use your leftover spinach! You can serve it for breakfast, lunch, dinner or even brunch. Marvelously elegant.

Servings: 2

Preparation Time: 5 minutes

Ingredients:

- 2 tbsp. butter
- ½ c. sliced mushrooms
- 3 cloves garlic, minced
- 14 oz. fresh baby spinach
- 1 dash nutmeg
- Salt and pepper to taste
- ¼ c. heavy cream
- ¼ c. grated parmesan cheese
- 6 eggs

Directions:

1. Melt the butter in a skillet.

2. Sauté the mushrooms and garlic for 2 minutes.

3. Add the spinach and nutmeg and stir for 3 minutes, until spinach has wilted.

4. Season with salt and pepper.

5. Next, stir in the heavy cream and grated cheese until the cheese has melted, about 2 minutes.

6. Pour half the sauce on a platter.

7. Next, bring 3 inches of salted water to boil in a pan.

8. Slide in the eggs and cook for 3 minutes.

9. Then, use a slotted spoon to transfer the eggs on top of the sauce.

10. Cover with the remaining sauce.

Fried Eggs and Shrimp

Your go-to scrambled egg mixes might not be added with shrimp, but once you try this recipe, you'll question why you've never done it before. Add some shrimp to an ordinary fried egg to make a delicious meal. You can serve the dish with a side of toast or even with a tortilla.

Servings: 3

Preparation Time: 35 minutes

Ingredients:

- 1 tbsp. vegetable oil, or as needed
- 1/4 c. cocktail sauce
- 1 onion, chopped
- 6 eggs, beaten
- 1 tsp. salt
- 10 cooked large shrimps

Directions:

1. Fry onions in hot oil for 11 mins. Then, mix in the eggs and salt. Continue frying for 6 minutes.

2. Add in your shrimp and cocktail sauce and continue to cook for 5 more minutes.

3. Enjoy.

Omelet

The great thing about omelets is that you can fill them with just about anything and turn them into a filling and hardy meal. This is a really quick and easy recipe when you're looking for something different to make for breakfast. Undoubtedly, you can eat it any time of the day, and it's delicious!

Servings: 2

Preparation Time: 6 minutes

Ingredients:

- 2 tbsp. butter
- 6 beaten eggs
- 1 tbsp. milk
- Salt and pepper to taste
- 4 slices cheese of choice
- 2 tbsp. chopped onions
- 4 slices tomato

Directions:

1. Combine the eggs with the milk, 1 tbsp. of onion, salt and pepper.

2. Pour half the egg mixture into the skillet and swirl the mixture around.

3. When the eggs begin to firm, add 2 slices of cheese and two tomato slices to one half of the omelet.

4. Cook for another 2 minutes and flip the other half over the fillings.

5. Slide the omelet onto a plate.

6. Repeat for the 2nd omelet.

Cheesy Broccoli and Onion Quiche

A snap to make, this simple vegetarian quiche looks fantastic on the table. This is a delicious and filling dish. You can use whatever vegetables you have on hand, but it's all delicious and easy to prepare.

Servings: 8

Preparation Time: 1 hour and 10 minutes

Ingredients:

- 2 tbsp. olive oil
- 1/3 c. shallots, chopped
- 1 tbsp. garlic, minced
- 2 c. fresh broccoli, chopped
- 1 (9 inches) pie crust, unbaked
- 1/4 c. mozzarella cheese, shredded
- 1/4 c. cheddar cheese, grated
- 6 whole eggs
- 4 egg whites
- 2/3 c. milk
- 1 tbsp. butter, melted
- Salt and freshly ground black pepper

Directions:

1. Preheat and set your oven to 350 F (175 C).

2. Heat oil in a large non-stick pan or skillet over medium flame. Stir-fry the shallots and garlic for 2-3 minutes or until aromatic.

3. Add the broccoli; cook, stirring occasionally until soft.

4. Transfer the cooked vegetables into the pie crust. Sprinkle with cheddar and mozzarella.

5. Whisk the eggs and stir in milk and melted butter in a medium bowl. Season to taste.

6. Pour the egg mixture over broccoli and cheese. Then, bake in the oven for 30 to 40 minutes, or until center has set fully.

7. Cool the quiche slightly before serving.

8. Enjoy.

Chipotle Bacon and Eggs

This is a delicious recipe that you can enjoy for breakfast, lunch, or dinner. You can serve the dish with a side of veggies if you want to keep it healthy.

Servings: 4

Preparation Time: 40 minutes

Ingredients:

- 4 slices bacon, chopped
- 3 vine-ripened tomatoes, chopped
- 6 eggs
- 1 avocado, peeled, pitted, and chopped
- 2 tbsp. sour cream
- 1 (6 oz.) package fresh spinach
- 1 tbsp. oil, or as needed
- 1/2 c. shredded Cheddar cheese
- 1 tbsp. chipotle-flavored hot sauce (such salt and ground black pepper to taste as Tabasco(R) Chipotle Pepper Sauce)

Directions:

1. Get a bowl, evenly mix sour cream and eggs.

2. Fry your bacon for 11 minutes. Then, remove oil excess with some paper towels.

3. Now you want to cook your eggs in oil in a frying pan for 7 minutes with your hot sauce.

4. Add in your spinach, avocadoes and tomatoes and cook for 1 more minute.

5. Finally, top everything with cheddar and a bit more pepper and salt. Let the cheese melt with another 0.5 to 1 minute of cooking time.

Avocado Egg Salad

This is a great dish to make if you want something else out of your leftover eggs. It's quick and easy to prepare, and it tastes great!

Servings: 2

Preparation Time: 30 minutes

Ingredients:

- 4 hard-boiled eggs, chopped
- ½ avocado, peeled and diced
- 2 tbsp. readymade mustard
- 2 stalks celery, finely chopped
- 1 tsp. salt
- 1 tsp. black pepper
- 1 tsp. garlic powder

Directions:

1. Place all ingredients in a large bowl and mix until thoroughly combined. Serve and enjoy.

Breakfast Eggs from India

Two eggs with your favorite spices will make the perfect meal. You can use all of the spices you have in your kitchen. This is a yummy and full of protein recipe, and it's healthy.

Servings: 2

Preparation Time: 20 minutes

Ingredients:

- 1/4 c. vegetable oil
- 3 green chili peppers, sliced
- 1 tsp. garam masala
- 2 large eggs
- 1 tsp. ground turmeric
- 1 tsp. ground coriander
- Salt to taste
- 1/2 c. finely chopped onion

Directions:

1. Get a bowl and add your eggs to it. Then, whisk them.

2. In a frying pan, cook the following in hot oil for 6 minutes: salt, green chili peppers, garam masala, onions, coriander, and turmeric.

3. After 6 minutes, pour in your eggs to the seasoned onions and chilies and scramble for 5 minutes.

Paprika Egg Salad

This is an absolutely delicious dish! Eggs and paprika are great together, and you can serve the dish with a side of toast.

Servings: 8

Preparation Time: 20 minutes

Ingredients:

- 8 hard-cooked eggs, chopped
- 1/4 tsp. paprika
- 1/4 c. plain fat-free yogurt
- 1/4 tsp. salt
- 1 tbsp. parsley flakes
- 1/4 tsp. onion powder

Directions:

1. To make this salad get a bowl: and combine all the ingredients until completely smooth and even.

2. Enjoy with toasted bread.

Chicken Egg Salad

This is a great dish to make if you're looking for something different to make for lunch or dinner. If you like pickles, try this recipe. One who appreciates an egg salad will enjoy chicken as well.

Servings: 7

Preparation Time: 1 hour and 30 minutes

Ingredients:

- 2 large chicken breasts, cooked and chopped
- 5 hard-boiled eggs, chopped
- 2 tbsp. onion, diced
- 2 stalks celery, diced
- 1 tsp. salt
- ½ tsp. black pepper
- 1 tsp. garlic powder
- 1 tbsp. green pepper, diced
- 2 tsp. sugar
- 2 c. mayonnaise

Directions:

1. Place all ingredients in a large bowl and mix until completely combined.

2. Chill at least 1 hour before serving. Serve and enjoy.

Gherkins Egg Salad

This is an unusual egg salad recipe, but it tastes great. It's quick and easy to prepare. The classic egg salad can be combined with gherkins. The recipe is splendid!

Servings: 4

Preparation Time: 25 minutes

Ingredients:

- 8 hard-boiled eggs, chopped
- ½ c. mayonnaise
- ¼ c. green onions, chopped
- 2 tbsp. chopped celery, or to taste
- 1 tbsp. chopped gherkins, or to taste
- ¼ tsp. brown mustard
- ¼ tsp. dry mustard
- ¼ tsp. paprika
- Salt and black pepper to taste

Directions:

1. Place all ingredients in a large bowl and mix until completely combined.

2. Serve and enjoy.

Easy Spicy Eggs

If you're looking for a way to spice up your eggs, this recipe is perfect! It's quick and easy to prepare, and it tastes great.

Servings: 4

Preparation Time: 20 minutes

Ingredients:

- 2 hard-cooked eggs, cut in half lengthwise
- 1 tbsp. cream-style horseradish sauce

Directions:

1. Take your eggs and take out the yolks. Put the yolks aside in a bowl.

2. Add horseradish to the yolks and mix everything evenly.

3. Simply fill each egg white with the yolk mix and chill before serving them.

Buttery Eggs

A delicious way to serve eggs for breakfast, lunch, or dinner. You can make this dish as is or with your favorite ingredients.

Servings: 3-4

Preparation Time: 30 minutes

Ingredients:

- 6 eggs
- 1/8 tsp. ground white pepper, if desired
- 2 tbsp. butter
- Salt and pepper to taste
- 2 tbsp. all-purpose flour
- 2 c. milk

Directions:

1. Get a big saucepan and fill it with water. Add your eggs to the water and bring it to a rolling boil. Once boiling for about a minute, then remove the pan from the heat and place a lid on it. Let it stand for about 13 mins.

2. After 13 minutes, take out the eggs, remove the shells, and dice them.

3. Now drain the saucepan of its water and melt some butter in it. Once the butter is melted, add some flour and heat it until a ball-like shape begins to form. Then, add in your milk and lightly stir until the sauce begins to boil.

4. While boiling, add in: salt, white pepper, chopped eggs, and black pepper. Heat everything up, then remove it all from the heat.

5. Enjoy with your favorite toasted bread.

Chicken Ham Pepper and Cheese Omelette

You can make this dish with leftover cooked chicken and cheese, or get a head start and cook them fresh. You can also add your favorite veggies to the recipe.

Servings: 4

Preparation Time: 20 minutes

Ingredients:

- 3 whole eggs
- 3 egg whites
- 2 tbsp. olive oil, divided
- 1/2 medium red bell pepper, diced
- 1/2 medium green bell pepper, diced
- 4 oz. chicken ham, diced
- 2 tbsp. green onion, chopped
- 2 tbsp. cheddar cheese, grated
- Freshly ground black pepper, to taste

Directions:

1. First, in a medium bowl, beat the eggs together and season to taste.

2. Heat 1 tbsp. of oil in a skillet or non-stick pan over medium flame. Stir-fry the red and green bell pepper until soft.

3. Add the chicken ham and cook for another 2 minutes. Transfer mixture to a clean plate. Set aside.

4. Next, in the same pan, add the remaining 1 tbsp. of oil. Then, pour the beaten egg and cook for about 2 minutes. Gently lift the edge of the egg mixture with a spatula, let the uncooked egg mixture flow to the edges of the pan. Cook for about 2 minutes.

5. Top half of the egg with chicken ham and vegetable mixture. Sprinkle with green onion. Slowly lift the other side over the ham and vegetable mixture. Sprinkle with cheese and cook further 1-2 minutes.

6. Then, transfer to a serving dish.

7. Serve and enjoy.

Simply the Best Egg Salad

Never stray from a classic egg salad because it is simply the best. If you're looking for a quick and easy way to make egg salad, this recipe is definitely for you. It's easy to prepare, and it tastes great!

Servings: 3

Preparation Time: 2 hours and 10 minutes

Ingredients:

- 4 hard-boiled eggs, chopped
- 2 tbsp. plain non-fat yogurt
- 1 tsp. Dijon mustard
- 2 tbsp. light mayonnaise
- 1 chopped green onion, optional
- ¼ c. celery, diced
- Salt and black pepper to taste

Directions:

1. Place all ingredients in a large bowl and mix until completely combined.

Quick Pickled Eggs with Beets

This is a quick pickled egg recipe that you can make ahead of time. It tastes great with cold dishes, as well as with hot dishes.

Servings: 8

Preparation Time: 10 minutes

Ingredients:

- 8 peeled hard-boiled eggs
- 15 oz. canned sliced beets, liquid reserved
- 4 oz. white vinegar
- 4 oz. white sugar
- 4 oz. water
- 1/2 tsp. cinnamon, ground

Directions:

1. Place peeled eggs in a glass jar with a lid.

2. Combine the rest of the ingredients in a saucepan and bring to a boil. Then, stir until sugar dissolves. Pour the mixture over the eggs in the jar and seal the container. Chill for 1-2 days before serving.

Scrambled Eggs with Tomato and Paprika

These eggs are perfect for brunch or lunch. They are a deliciously distinct brunch dish, but easy enough to make them almost every day! You can also enjoy them as a side dish to meals.

Servings: 4

Preparation Time: 20 minutes

Ingredients:

- 4 whole eggs
- 2 egg whites
- 3 tbsp. sour cream
- 2 tbsp. olive oil
- 1/3 c. shallots, chopped
- 1 tsp. garlic, minced
- 2 medium tomatoes, chopped
- 2 tsp. sweet paprika, divided
- Salt and freshly ground black pepper

Directions:

1. First, in a medium bowl, whisk together the eggs and sour cream.

2. Heat oil in a large non-stick pan or skillet over medium flame. Add the shallots and garlic, stir-fry for 2-3 minutes or until aromatic.

3. Add the tomatoes and 1 teaspoon paprika; cook for 2-3 minutes, stirring occasionally.

4. Next, pour the egg mixture into the pan; cook, stirring often for 2-3 minutes or to desired doneness. Season to taste.

5. Then, transfer to a serving dish. Sprinkle with remaining 1 teaspoon of paprika.

6. Serve and enjoy.

Curried Deviled Eggs

This is a delicious and filling dish. You can use any vegetables you have in your fridge, depending on what you have available. Add a bit of exotic flavor to your deviled eggs with a dash of curry.

Servings: 6

Preparation Time: 8 minutes

Ingredients:

- 6 eggs
- 2 tbsp. mayonnaise
- 1 tsp. ground mustard
- 1 tsp. curry powder
- 1 dash marjoram
- 1 tbsp. chopped black olives
- Salt and pepper to taste
- 1 tbsp. minced celery
- Garnish with sweet paprika

Directions:

1. Boil the eggs according to the boiled egg instructions.

2. When the eggs have cooled, slice the eggs horizontally and spoon out the yolks.

3. Mash the yolks and combine with mayonnaise, mustard, curry powder, marjoram, salt and pepper.

4. Spoon the filling in the egg-white halves. Garnish with paprika.

Cloud Eggs

If you're looking for a great brunch recipe, this is a great option. You can serve the delicious eggs with a side of veggies or falafel. They're quick and easy to make.

Servings: 2

Preparation Time: 5 minutes

Ingredients:

- 2 egg whites
- 2 egg yolks
- 1 tsp. grated Gruyere cheese
- 1 tsp. chopped chives
- Salt and pepper to taste

Directions:

1. Preheat the oven to 400 degrees.

2. Cover a baking sheet with parchment paper.

3. Whip the egg whites, cheese, chives, salt and pepper until fluffy.

4. Arrange two egg white heaps on the baking sheet.

5. Bake for 3 minutes.

6. Take the baking sheet out of the oven and gently slide 1 egg yolk onto each heap.

7. Return the eggs to the oven and bake for another 3 minutes.

French Toast

French toast is a classic dish that you can eat for breakfast, brunch or lunch. You can serve this delicious egg recipe with a side of fruit.

Servings: 6

Preparation Time: 10 minutes per slice

Ingredients:

- 3 eggs
- ¾ c. milk
- 2 tbsp. brown sugar
- ¼ tsp. cinnamon
- 1 tsp. vanilla extract
- 3 tbsp. butter
- 6 slices Texas Toast bread
- ¼ c. maple syrup

Directions:

1. Whisk together all ingredients except the bread.

2. Dip (don't soak) each bread slice in the egg mixture.

3. Melt the butter in a skillet.

4. Cook the bread slices 5 minutes on each side or until golden brown.

5. Top with maple syrup.

Spinach Quiche

This is a great recipe if you're looking for something different to make for breakfast. You can serve it with a side of fruit and vegetables if you want to keep it healthy. Quiche is always an excellent use of eggs. Serve the quiche with a side of bacon or sausages.

Servings: 6

Preparation Time: 40 minutes

Ingredients:

- 1 frozen pie crust
- 2 tbsp. olive oil
- 5 oz. fresh spinach
- 2 c. shredded Swiss cheese
- 1 c. sliced mushrooms
- 1 c. shredded mozzarella cheese
- 2 tbsp. chopped scallions
- 6 beaten eggs
- Salt and pepper to taste

Directions:

1. Preheat the oven to 350 degrees F.

2. Place the pie crust in the oven for 5 minutes to prevent it from getting soggy.

3. While the pie crust is browning, heat the olive oil in a skillet.

4. Sauté the spinach, mushrooms and scallions for 5 minutes. Drain any excess liquid.

5. Whisk the eggs and add to the vegetable mixture.

6. Season with salt and pepper.

7. Place the shredded cheese in the pie crust and pour in the eggs.

8. Bake for 30 minutes.

Vegetable Frittata

This is a delicious and healthy dish that you can serve with a side of fruit or simply with your favorite vegetables. It's quick and easy to prepare, so it's great for busy mornings. The frittata is filled with healthy goodness. Great for lunch or have with a salad for dinner.

Servings: 6

Preparation Time: 19 minutes

Ingredients:

- 3 tbsp. olive oil
- 1 tsp. Italian seasoning
- 1 dash cayenne pepper
- 6 small potatoes
- 1 c. diced red bell peppers
- ½ c. sliced mushrooms
- 1 diced and seeded tomato
- 1 c. torn fresh spinach
- 3 tbsp. chopped scallions
- 1 dash garlic powder
- Salt and pepper to taste
- 6 eggs
- 2/3 c. milk
- ¾ c. shredded Cheddar cheese

Directions:

1. Combine 1 tbsp. of olive oil with the Italian seasoning and cayenne pepper.

2. Slice the potatoes very thin and coat with the seasoning mix.

3. Heat 2 tbsps. of olive oil in a skillet.

4. Cook the seasoned potatoes, mushrooms and bell peppers for 10 minutes.

5. Stir in the spinach and scallion and season with salt, pepper and garlic powder.

6. Cook for 4 minutes.

7. Whisk the eggs and milk together. Then, add to the skillet.

8. Top with the shredded cheese.

9. Cook covered and on low for 5 minutes, or until the eggs have set.

Huevos Rancheros

If you're looking for a great dish to wake up with, try this recipe. You can make the dish any time of the day, and it's delicious.

Servings: 8

Preparation Time: 29 minutes

Ingredients:

- 8 corn tortillas
- 2 c. store-bought or homemade salsa
- 2 tsp. vegetable oil
- 1 small chopped onion
- 3 cloves garlic, minced
- 18 oz. drained black beans
- ¼ c. chicken broth
- 2 seeded and diced green chilis
- 1 c. shredded queso fresco cheese
- 8 eggs
- 3 oz. sour cream

Directions:

1. Preheat the oven to 375 degrees.

2. Next, wrap the tortillas in aluminum foil and heat for 5 minutes.

3. Heat 1 tbsp. of oil in a skillet.

4. Next, cook the onion and garlic for 5 minutes.

5. Add the beans, broth and diced chili.

6. Simmer for 10 minutes.

7. Remove from heat and keep warm. Keep the oven on.

8. Add the additional oil to the skillet. Scramble the eggs, about 4 minutes.

9. Then, top each heated tortilla with the black beans, some salsa and top with scrambled egg.

10. Cover each tortilla with the shredded cheese.

11. Place the tortillas on a baking sheet. Then, return to the oven.

12. Lastly, bake for 5 minutes or until cheese is bubbly. Serve with sour cream.

Beef Egg Salad

For all beef lovers, you can try this combination of beef with egg salad. If you're looking for a hearty dish that's quick and easy to make, you can try it. You can use any vegetables you have on hand.

Servings: 4

Preparation Time: 45 minutes

Ingredients:

- 4 hard-boiled eggs, chopped
- ¾ lb. skirt steak, cooked
- 1 head romaine lettuce, separated leaves
- 1 head radicchio, separated leaves
- 1 lb. tomatoes, cut into wedges
- 1 small red onion, thinly sliced
- 3 tbsp. extra- virgin olive oil
- 2 tbsp. Sherry or red wine vinegar
- Salt and black pepper to taste

Directions:

1. Season the steak with black pepper and salt. Then, cook to medium rare. Once done, let it rest for 5 minutes and cut against the grain.

2. Divide the lettuce, radicchio, tomatoes, steak, onion, and eggs into four plates. Whisk the vinegar and the olive oil into a bowl. Pour the dressing on each plate of salad. Serve and enjoy.

Breakfast Biscuits

These breakfast biscuits are far superior to ones from fast food places. If you're looking for a different way to enjoy biscuits, you can try this recipe. It's quick and easy to make, and it tastes amazing!

Servings: 6

Preparation Time: 10 minutes

Ingredients:

- 6 homemade or frozen biscuits
- 12 slices Swiss or cheddar cheese
- 1 lb. breakfast sausage
- 6 eggs
- 3 tbsp. milk
- Pepper and salt to taste
- 2 tbsp. butter

Directions:

1. Preheat your oven to 350 degrees.

2. Split the biscuits in two and top each half with a slice of cheese.

3. Next, place the biscuits on a baking tray and bake for 5 minutes, until the cheese melts.

4. While the cheese is melting, heat the butter in a skillet.

5. Combine the eggs with the milk and season with salt and pepper.

6. Next, pour the eggs into the skillet and scramble for 5 minutes.

7. Transfer the eggs to a plate and keep warm.

8. Then, use the same skillet to fry the sausage for minutes. Remove the biscuits from the oven. Each biscuit half should have melted cheese.

9. Top four biscuit halves with sausage and eggs. Top with the remaining biscuit halves to create sandwiches.

Smoked Salmon Egg Salad

This is a delicious and healthy recipe that's a great alternative to the traditional egg salad. You can make the dish with hard-boiled eggs, which are easier to prepare.

Servings: 8

Preparation Time: 30 minutes

Ingredients:

- 12 hard-boiled eggs, chopped
- 2 stalks celery, chopped
- 1 red onion, diced
- 5 oz. smoked salmon, diced
- 3 tbsp. fresh dill, chopped
- Salt and black pepper to taste
- 1 c. mayonnaise
- 4 small seedless cucumber

Directions:

1. Place all ingredients in a large bowl and mix until completely combined.

2. Chill in a refrigerator for 2 hours or more. Serve and enjoy.

Chakchouka

This is an easy dish to make if you're looking for something different. It's quick and easy to prepare, and it tastes great!

Servings: 4

Preparation Time: 30 minutes

Ingredients:

- 1 tbsp. olive oil
- ½ lb. ground sausage meat
- 1 chopped onion
- 1 sliced red bell pepper
- 3 cloves garlic, minced
- 14 oz. can diced tomatoes
- 1 tsp. cumin
- ½ c. fresh cilantro
- ½ tsp. salt
- 1 seeded and chopped jalapeno pepper
- 4 eggs

Directions:

1. Heat the olive oil in a skillet.

2. Brown the sausage for 5 minutes.

3. Next, add the onion, bell pepper and garlic and cook for another 5 minutes.

4. Stir in the diced tomatoes, cumin, salt and jalapeno pepper and combine well.

5. Season with cumin and salt.

6. Simmer for 15 minutes.

7. Crack the eggs into the tomato sauce.

8. Then, place a lid on the skillet and cook for 5 minutes until the eggs are soft but done.

9. Place the eggs on a platter and top with cilantro.

10. Serve with toast.

Mustard Pickled Eggs

This is a quick and easy recipe that can be prepared in 10 minutes. You can serve them with a side of veggies if you want to keep them healthy.

Servings: 6

Preparation Time: 5 minutes

Ingredients:

- 6 peeled hard-boiled eggs
- 1/2 tsp. mustard powder
- ¼ oz. cornstarch
- 1 tsp. white sugar
- 1/2 tsp. turmeric, ground
- 1 tsp. salt
- 16 oz. apple cider vinegar

Directions:

1. Place eggs in a 32-oz. jar.

2. Combine mustard, cornstarch, sugar, salt and turmeric in a pan and add enough vinegar to make a paste with the mixture. Add the rest of the vinegar and bring to a boil. Stir often.

3. Pour the mixture over the eggs in the jar and seal the container with a lid. Chill for 3-4 days before serving.

Irresistible Scotch Eggs

You can make these delicious eggs in as little as 45 minutes. They're great for a quick and healthy snack, or they can be served with an egg salad, tomato and avocado sandwich.

Servings: 6

Preparation Time: 45 minutes

Ingredients:

- 6 eggs with shells + 1 beaten egg
- 1 lb. ground sausage
- 1 tbsp. mustard
- 2 tsp. corn flour
- 1 tbsp. Worcestershire sauce
- ¼ tsp. mace powder
- 2 sprigs thyme, finely chopped
- 2 leaves sage, finely chopped
- Salt and pepper to taste
- Oil for deep frying
- ¼ c. milk
- ½ c. flour
- 2 c. fresh bread crumbs

Directions:

1. Cover 6 eggs with water in a saucepan and bring it to a boil. Take off the heat, cover and let it remain for 6 minutes. Now, transfer eggs to a bowl of chilled water and leave it for 5 more minutes before draining and peeling.

2. In another bowl, mix the rest of the ingredients except the last three ingredients and the beaten egg. Divide this mixture into 6 portions and wrap each portion around the egg. Refrigerate for half hour.

3. Meanwhile, heat oil in the wok over medium heat. Beat the beaten egg with milk in a bowl and keep the last two ingredients in separate bowls. Coat the prepared eggs with flour followed by egg and then finally by breadcrumbs. Deep fry for 5 minutes, drain and let them cool before serving.

Egg Salad Sandwiches

You must have heard of boiled egg sandwiches with tea, but here is something more delicious that you can try. If you're looking for a great lunch or dinner option, try this meaty egg salad sandwich. It tastes great with a side of veggies.

Servings: 3-4

Preparation Time: 10-12 minutes

Ingredients:

- 6 eggs, large
- 8 slices whole wheat bread, toasted
- 2 tbsp. mayonnaise or Greek yogurt
- 1 tsp. lemon juice
- Salt and pepper to taste
- ½ bunch chives, chopped
- 2 stalks celery, chopped
- 1 bunch lettuce leaves

Directions:

1. To boil the eggs, place them in a pot filled with water that comes just ½ inch above the eggs. Then, put the pot on medium heat and bring it to boil gently. Turn off the heat, cover the pot and leave it like that for 7 minutes. After 7 minutes, dip the eggs in ice cold water in a bowl for a couple of minutes.

2. Peel the eggs, then place them in a mixing bowl. Add mayonnaise, salt and pepper and mash them up together. Add the chives and celery to the mixture.

3. To assemble the sandwich, place a lettuce leaf on a toasted slice and a generous serving of egg mixture. Now finish it off by putting another slice over it.

Cheesy Egg Whites in a Mug

Only a few things are simpler and tastier than this dish. This is a great option if you're looking for a healthy breakfast option. It takes only 3 minutes to cook, so it's quick and easy!

Servings: 1

Preparation Time: 3 minutes

Ingredients:

- 2 egg whites
- 2 tbsp. reduced fat cheddar cheese, shredded
- 1 tbsp. milk
- 1/8 tsp. garlic salt
- 1/8 tsp. dried basil leaves
- Pepper to taste

Directions:

1. Take a double sized microwave-safe mug and grease it lightly. Add the whites, milk, half of cheese, salt, pepper and basil to it. Stir nicely with a fork. Microwave the mixture on high for a minute.

2. Take out, stir again and keep for half a minute more. Sprinkle more cheese and serve.

Conclusion

For individuals with a properly balanced diet, eggs are safe to eat and are not a cause for concern. At the same time, the protein in eggs is less than other protein sources, so you're best off eating a variety of sources. Make sure that you always get your nutrients from whole or minimally processed food instead of supplements. Most people are not deficient in dietary protein, and those who are will likely get enough from other sources like meat.

Omega 3 fatty acids found in eggs are necessary for heart and eye health. Eggs also contain vitamins A, D, E and B12, but they are not a source of iron as you would find in red meat. It is important to stay hydrated as water is a great way of flushing toxins out of your body and keeping your body running at its best.

The nutrients in eggs are found in other food, so it's important to get your vitamins from whole food rather than supplements. Eggs are a great source of protein and should be included as part of a well-balanced diet. They are also loaded with essential nutrients, which are essential for your health. Eggs are cholesterol-free and should be eaten in moderation.

It is best to use omega 3 eggs when preparing your diet; however, you can still eat regular eggs when following a healthy eating plan. You can also eat eggs on a regular basis, even if you are trying to lose weight. It is best to be aware of what you are eating so that you and your family can remain healthy and happy!

I can't tell you how grateful I am that you decided to read my book. My most heartfelt thanks that you took time out of your life to choose my work, and I hope you find benefit within the pages. So, from this, I bid you farewell in your egg journey, stay safe, and enjoy the recipes!

Author's Afterthoughts

Thanks ever so much to each of my cherished readers for investing the time to read this book!

I know you could have picked from many other books, but you chose this one. So, a big thanks for reading all the way to the end. If you enjoyed this book or received value from it, I'd like to ask you for a favor. Please take a few minutes to **post an honest and heartfelt review on *Amazon.com*.** Your support does make a difference and helps to benefit other people.

Thanks!

Julia Chiles

Printed in Great Britain
by Amazon